T0014348

Edgar Degas

Dance like
a Butterfly

Angela Wenzel

Prestel
Munich · London · New York

Edgar Degas never got bored watching ballet! But it wasn't as if he had ever wanted to become a dancer himself. His great love was painting.

Degas wanted to bring movement into his pictures and to paint the surprising and exciting moments of life in Paris as it was when he lived there 130 years ago. The stage lighting, the rooms behind the wings which the audience never saw, the figures and steps the ballerinas danced, and the materials from which the costumes were made all fascinated the artist.

But it was not just the public performances that Degas found interesting. In fact he could best watch the dancers when they were practicing. He studied every detail very closely and made quick sketches in his little pad of paper. He used these drawings later in his studio as the basis for his paintings.

Degas also painted other subjects, but it was his pictures of ballet dancers that really made him famous. Nobody else had ever painted them so brilliantly before. Thousands of drawings and pictures of ballet scenes piled up in his studio— and he even owned a silk ballet shoe that was a great help when he was painting.

The ballet shoe that Degas once owned

*The dancer is listening carefully to her teacher while the violinist,
who always played at rehearsals, is concentrating on the music*

*B*allet was still very much in fashion when Degas was living in Paris. There were no televisions or cinemas at that time and ballet performances in the Opera House were box office hits like the best movies today. This meant that it was not difficult for Degas to sell his pictures of dancers at all—he was really very lucky! Although he came from a rich family of bankers, the bank had lost all its money after his father's death and the artist was left with very little.

It was not surprising that ballet was still so popular in Paris. It had had a long tradition starting some two hundred years earlier during the reign of King Louis XIV who particularly liked ballet. He even used to join in the dancing himself! In 1653 he danced the part of the sun in a royal ballet performance, which was very fitting since he was later known as "The Sun King." He went on to found the Royal Academy of Music and Dance that became the Royal School of Opera in 1712. Not just the children from rich, aristocratic families were allowed to attend the school; talented boys and girls who came from poor families went there, too, and were taught free of charge.

The Opera House in Paris around 1900

In 1875, a new and very impressive opera house was opened in Paris and it soon became the meeting place for all opera and ballet fans. Degas could go in and out of the building as he pleased and knew every little nook and cranny of the new building. He mixed with the musicians as well so that he could watch the dancing on stage from a different angle, as we can see in this painting.

The bright costumes of the dancers are very different from the dark jackets worn by the musicians in the orchestra

It was only very seldom that Degas painted scenes from an actual ballet that he had seen. However, the ballet scene in *Robert le Diable* was different. 'Robert the Devil' was the name given to the Duke of Normandy, the father of the famous king, William the Conqueror, who lived in the eleventh century. There are many legends about the duke. In the opera, he is made out to be the son of the Devil who is getting him ready for his life in Hell. However, Robert falls in love with a princess and it all ends up happily ever after.

Although the painting has been given the same name as the ballet, it isn't really possible to recognize any particular scene in Degas' painting. He didn't feel that this was important. Instead he wanted to show the contrast between the people sitting quietly in their dark suits in the audience and the actors dancing in their brilliant white, flowing robes on stage. The musical instruments provide a link between the two halves of the painting. The artist also painted the effects of the lighting very carefully, picking out the white collars of the men's shirts as well as the costumes.

Degas would probably have known a number of these musicians and opera fans

Monsieur Jules Perrot was an excellent dancer when he was young. He then went on to make a name for himself as a choreographer. A choreographer is someone who matches the dancers' steps to music.

I wonder if the young girl on the piano really dared to sit there scratching her back while her teacher was looking! Monsieur Perrot was a very strict teacher. He used to wave the stick he is leaning on around wildly whenever anyone was not paying attention. Nothing ever went unnoticed! It may be that Degas had sketched the tired ballerina earlier when she was standing in the wings and then painted her into his picture of the dance class sometime later. The artist didn't actually take his paints and easel along to the Opera House but put his paintings together in his studio using sketches he had made of the dancers in various poses.

Degas soon got to know lots of musicians, ballet teachers, and dancers. Louis-Amédée Mante was a musician in the Opera House orchestra and lived for a while in the same building as Degas. His three daughters all went to ballet class and so it was that, together with their mother—shown below with Suzanne and Blanche—the children came to be the artist's models.

Suzanne went on to become a ballet teacher herself. She remembered well how closely Degas watched the ballerinas running up and down the stairs in the Opera House. Now and then he would ask them to freeze for a moment so that he could sketch them quickly. She had fond memories of the kind, elderly artist.

But not everyone thought well of him! Many people knew Degas as a grumpy, stingy old man. He certainly had a mind of his own. He had very unusual ideas for his paintings and had to have peace and quiet in order to be able to work.

Suzanne Mante, here in her ballet dress, was seven years old when Degas painted this picture. Her younger sister, Blanche, doesn't look very happy. Perhaps she wanted to play outside rather than having to go to her dancing lesson

Training to be a ballet dancer in those days called for a lot of hard work and practise, just as it does today. The children had lessons from nine until one o'clock, followed by three hours of rehearsals. All those who were performing in the evening then had to appear on stage with a smile on their face as if they had had a quiet and relaxing day. Depending on how talented the dancers were, some fourteen to sixteen-year-olds were even allowed to take on major roles.

Not everybody was as lucky as the Mante children. Some of the dancers were from very poor families and always seemed to be hungry. But whether they were rich or poor, they all danced like butterflies when on stage.

Two mothers with their daughters who are waiting for the dancing exam to begin

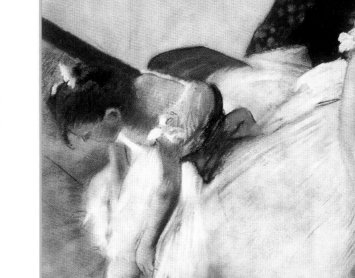

Practice makes perfect

Many mothers went along with their daughters to dance classes. These ladies, who Degas often painted in darker colors, provided a perfect contrast to the young ballerinas. This makes the dancers look even more delicate and graceful in their light-colored dresses.

The lady in the straw hat is reading a paper while waiting. Although she is not the main person in the painting, she is pictured in the foreground. Our eyes pass over her to the girl with the long hair and the dancing teacher next to her. Then our gaze is drawn towards the young pupils practicing their steps very carefully on the left of the picture.

*D*egas knew this cheeky little dancer personally. She's called Marie van Goethem and was the model the artist drew for a number of different pictures.

Degas looked closely at how Marie was standing and then drew her in pencil. She may be about to do what is known as the fourth position in classical ballet or she may just be limbering up.

Degas also made figures out of wax, but it took more than ten years before he decided to put them on display. *The Little Fourteen-Year-Old Dancer*, which he had made based on drawings and from working with Marie, was first shown in an exhibition in 1881.

Degas painted Marie's portrait many times. He always said that he liked to paint the same person or thing "ten times or a hundred times. Nothing in art must look as if it is accidental, not even movement."

This wax figure caused quite a stir! The dancer had a funny little nose and actually looked like a real girl rather than a pretty butterfly. Degas also dressed her in a skirt made of tulle with a bodice of real silk. She even had a ribbon in her hair and had satin ballet shoes on her feet. This was something very new at that time. Real things were not normally added to sculptures. But opinions about the little ballerina differed. Some found her "absolutely hideous," while others said that Degas had paid "careful attention to all the details" and that she looked very lifelike.

After Edgar Degas' death the wax model was used to make a series of some twenty-eight bronze figures. These were fitted with real clothes and can now be seen in many of the biggest museums in America and Europe. Marie herself didn't become a famous ballerina. But she did become world famous as *The Little Fourteen-Year-Old Dancer*.

The Little Fourteen-Year-Old Dancer *is one of Degas' most famous works*

Just imagine how nervous the pupils must have been before going on stage for the final rehearsal. Nobody would have been sitting in the audience—it was just a huge empty space, or so they thought. But there were certainly a few people watching secretly from the shadows. Degas must have been there too, and captured the atmosphere of the stage rehearsals and their magical lighting effects in several paintings.

The men sitting in the background during rehearsals always kept a lookout for talented young dancers who went on to become the stars of the stage

It's fun to look at both of these pictures more closely. Many of these figures turn up in more than one painting. This helps us understand how Degas worked: he used to watch the dancers when they were having their lessons, at rehearsals and during performances. He made lots of sketches, looking carefully at how the dancers were standing. When he got back to his studio, he would then group the figures together against backgrounds that were not exact copies of the original rooms but were made up from all sorts of different things that he had seen.

W hen painting the dancers on the right, Degas didn't have to ask four different dancers to model for him, but just one! And, instead of using sketches, he painted the picture from photographs he had taken himself in his studio.

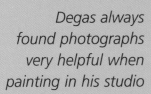

The photographs are very interesting. Using a special method Degas made the light and dark areas look very much like the shadows cast by the gas lights on the stage.

Degas always found photographs very helpful when painting in his studio

The poises may be part of a graceful pirouette. Degas was after all very interested in the experimental pictures taken by the famous photographer Eadweard Muybridge. In 1873, Muybridge became the first person to take photographs of galloping horses, running animals and people dancing or doing exercise. His photographs showed each different movement one after another, like a film in slow motion. His photographs attracted a lot of attention because, up until then, nobody had really known, for example, exactly how a horse's legs move when it is running.

Dancers like butterflies caught in a mass of color and light

E dgar Degas always tried to paint familiar things from different angles and to show their unusual side in a way no one had ever seen before. Photography, which was something very new at that time, was a welcome and exciting way of making people look at the world around them in a different way. He seemed to have had lots of fun taking pictures with his camera.

Who hasn't accidentally cut out someone's hand when taking a photograph, or chopped off a person's feet or even a head? These photographic "mistakes" gave Degas an idea. He picked up on these pictures to make some of his paintings more interesting. The picture on the right, for instance, seems to have caught the dancers in different positions as if by chance—just as if he had taken a quick snapshot. If you look a little more closely you will see that the artist has built up the picture very carefully and cleverly. The brown-colored paneling on the left forms an excellent contrast to the girls in their brightly-colored dresses. The ballerina whose nose and hand cannot be seen, makes us curious for more and our eye is automatically drawn to the other dancer.

*A ballerina reading all about yesterday
evening's performance in a Paris newspaper*

Let's take another look behind the scenes. This was not the picture the Parisians had of the butterfly-like ballerinas they watched on stage!

This everyday scene, which hardly anybody ever got to see, shows a dancer next to a big, dark stove. When the ballerinas had a break, they had to be very careful that they didn't catch a chill. It almost seems as if the stove is watching the girl reading a newspaper! Its heavy, simple shape is very different from the delicate figure in the light-colored dress.

On the right is another unusual view which no ordinary ballet fan would ever have seen. "Is my silk choker alright?" the young girl in pink seems to be asking, while the other dancer in the turquoise dress is thinking about something before going on stage. Or do you think that the two dancers have already finished their performance? Perhaps they are really tired and the one girl is loosening her choker while the other is still lost in her thoughts. For Degas the structure of the painting was more important than the answer to such questions. He clearly shows us two figures in the foreground moving apart, one to the left, the other to the right, and outlines a row of dancers in the background.

The delicate materials of the glittering and colorful costumes made Degas want to add lots of exciting colors in his paintings

Degas never painted any ballet scenes from directly in front of the stage as if the dancers had lined up for a photograph for a local newspaper.

In the painting on the right we can see the dancers on stage, but some are shown from behind, over the heads of the musicians in the orchestra pit.

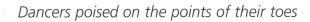

Dancers poised on the points of their toes

What do you think has caught everyone's attention?
They don't seem to be looking at the dancers on stage at all!

Degas reworked a black-and-white print for this picture by adding colored pastel. At first, the picture above would have looked like the small image on the left. Degas covered a glass plate with black ink, then wiped some of it away with a brush or a cloth to uncover the figures. When a print was made the figures appeared in white against a black background. This was a very good way to create the magic effect of the stage lighting. When he wanted to print the figures in black on a white background, he painted and drew in black on a clear glass plate.

This mixture of material and paint captures the magic of ballet. This pure silk fan has been painted using a type of watercolor, gold, and charcoal.

In those days, Europeans were just becoming interested in the art and culture of Japan and Japanese fans were soon very much in fashion

Degas very much liked working in pastel for pictures like the one on the right in which the colors have a lovely velvet-like glow. Degas put one layer of pastel on another in order to fill his pictures with light and color. He then added spots of paint to certain areas. He reworked his paintings time and time again, often over a period of several years, until he was finally satisfied with the result.

In the picture on the right, Degas lets us watch the performance as if we were sitting in the same box at the side of the stage as the lady in the lovely sequin dress. Together with others in the audience, we can look over her shoulder and marvel at the pretty ballerina in her yellow dress.

Ladies never went to the opera without their fan or their opera glasses. They could then see every little detail and also have a good look at other people in the audience

*I*t must be a dancer's dream to become a famous prima ballerina! What a feeling to take your bow after a performance to the sound of everyone clapping enthusiastically. One of the dancer's fans has given this ballerina a bouquet of flowers and everyone's eyes are fixed on the young girl. She is the star of the show, bathing in the bright lights that cast a shadow across her face. The orange umbrellas in the background cleverly pick up the color and shape of the skirt worn by the dancer coming onto the stage from the left.

Although ballet was very popular, there were very few truly great ballet stars at that time. French ballet had already had its heyday but just a few years before Degas' death, a lot of interest was being shown in ballet once again. Many new and famous dancers appeared on the scene, but none of them ever stood as a model for Degas. That didn't bother him in the least; after all, that wasn't the most important thing for him, was it?

Applause!

Just listen to the cheers and the clapping!

Edgar Degas' life

Edgar Degas was born on July 19, 1834, in Paris. His full name was Hilaire-Germain Edgar de Gas, but later on he wrote his last name as one word.

When he was eighteen, he set up an artist's studio in his parent's house. His father, who was a rich banker, wanted Edgar to study law after leaving school, but finally allowed his son to study art instead. It didn't take long for Degas to get to know a number of artists, some of whom, like himself, went on to become very famous and were known as the Impressionists. In 1878 Degas sold his first painting to a museum. By this time, he was working more and more in pastel chalk, but he also made models out of wax. Degas' model of the little fourteen-year-old dancer shown in this book could be seen at the sixth exhibition that the Impressionists held in 1881.

By this time the family bank was in trouble. Degas' father had died and the bank had lost huge sums on the stock exchange. The artist had to find a lot of money to pay back and the sale of his paintings became a very important source of income. His pictures often showed everyday scenes in Paris such as people at the races or in cafés, but he also painted certain activities, such as women doing the ironing or making hats. Most of all he painted pictures of ballet dancers from the Opera House in Paris.

As he got older, his eye-sight became increasingly poor but that didn't stop him from traveling a great deal. At the end of his life he was almost blind. Edgar Degas died on September 27, 1917, in Paris. On his tombstone in the family grave in the cemetery in Montmartre it says: "Drawing was his great love."

The Impressionists

The Impressionists didn't paint religious or historical subjects as was usual at that time, but instead they focused on everyday scenes. Painters such as Claude Monet and Auguste Renoir focused on color and showed the different effect that light has on objects. Things lost their hard outlines and paintings turned into color compositions. The artists didn't want to paint unnatural scenes any more. Instead they tried to paint things as they saw them at a particular moment. That's why many Impressionist paintings look like snapshots. This development in art was largely due to painters such as Edgar Degas and a friend of his, Edouard Manet.

The illustrations in this book

All the works pictured are by Edgar Degas

front cover: *Dancer Posing for the Photographer* (detail), *c.* 1879
Pushkin State Museum of Fine Arts, Moscow

back cover: *The Stage Rehearsal*, *c.* 1875
Nelson-Atkins Museum of Art, Kansas City

title page:
The Dance Class (detail), see page 9
Dancer Resting, *c.* 1879. Private collection

pages 2/3
bottom left: Ballet shoe once owned by Degas
right: *The Dance Foyer at the Opera on the rue Le Peletier*, 1872.
Museé d'Orsay, Paris

pages 4/5
left: The Opera House in Paris, *c.* 1900. Postcard
right: *Orchestra Musicians*, 1870–76. Städtische Galerie
im Städelschen Kunstinstitut, Frankfurt am Main

pages 6/7
left: *Dancer*, *c.* 1885. Galerie Jan Krugier, Geneva
right: *The Ballet Scene in* Robert le Diable, 1876
The Victoria and Albert Museum, London

pages 8/9
left: *The Mante Family*, *c.* 1889. Philadelphia Museum of Art,
Gift of Mrs. John Wintersteen
right: *The Dance Class*, 1873–75. Musée d'Orsay, Paris

pages 10/11
left: *The Dance Exam*, *c.* 1879. Denver Art Museum, Colorado
right: *The Ballet Class*, 1881. Philadelphia Museum of Art

pages 12/13
left: *Three Studies for a Dancer in the Fourth Position*, *c.* 1878–81
The Art Institute of Chicago, Bequest of Adele R. Levy (1062.703)
center: *Four Studies for a Dancer*, *c.* 1878–79. Musée du Louvre, Paris
right: *The Little Fourteen-Year-Old Dancer*, *c.* 1878–81
Collection of Mr. and Mrs. Paul Mellon, National Gallery of Art,
Washington

pages 14/15
left: *The Rehearsal Onstage*, 1874
The Metropolitan Museum of Art, New York
right: *Ballet Rehearsal on Stage*, 1874. Musée d'Orsay, Paris

pages 16/17
left: Two photographs of a dancer, both taken by Degas *c.* 1896
Bibliothèque Nationale de France, Paris
right: *Behind the Scenes*, *c.* 1898. Pushkin State Museum of Fine
Arts, Moscow

pages 18/19
left: *Dancer Sitting*, *c.* 1878. Musée du Louvre, Paris
right: *Dancers in the Wings*, *c.* 1878–80
The Norton Simon Museum of Art, Pasadena

pages 20/21
left: *Dancer Resting*, 1878–80. Private collection
right: *The Entrance of the Masked Dancers*, 1879–82. Sterling
and Francine Clark Art Institute, Williamstown, Massachusetts

pages 22/23
left: *Dancer Bending Forward*, 1874–79. The Art Institute of Chicago,
Mr. and Mrs. Martin A. Ryerson Collection
bottom: *Three Ballet Dancers*, *c.* 1876. Sterling and Francine Clark
Art Institute, Williamstown, Massachussetts
right: *Ballet at the Paris Opera*, 1877. The Art Institute of Chicago

pages 24/25
left: *Dancers (Fan-Design)*, *c.* 1879. The Baltimore Musuem
of Art, Fanny B. Thalheimer Memorial Fund (1963.9) Photography
By: Mitro Hood right: *Ballet from an Opera Box*, 1885. Philadelphia
Museum of Art, John G. Johnson Collection

pages 26/27
left: *Swaying Dancer (Dancer in Green)*, 1877–79. Fundación Collección
Thyssen-Bornemisza, Madrid
center: *The Box at the Opera House*, 1880. Private collection
right: *Dancer Bowing with Bouquet*, *c.* 1877. Musée d'Orsay, Paris

pages 28/29
left: Photograph by Degas, *c.* 1895
Bibliothèque Nationale de France, Paris
right: *Dancer*, 1873. Galerie Jan Krugier, Geneva

© 2023, Prestel Verlag,
Munich · London · New York
A member of Penguin Random House Verlagsgruppe GmbH
Neumarkter Strasse 28 · 81673 Munich

Library of Congress Control Number: 2023933371
A CIP catalogue record for this book is available from
the British Library.

Text and picture selection: Angela Wenzel
Translated from German by Rosie Jackson
Copyediting: Christopher Wynne
Design and layout: Susanne Rüber
Production management: Susanne Hermann
Lithography: ReproLine, Munich
Printing and binding: Printer Trento, Trento

Prestel Publishing compensates the CO_2 emissions produced from
the making of this book by supporting a reforestation project in
Brazil. Find further information on the project here:
www.ClimatePartner.com/14044-1912-1001

Penguin Random House Verlagsgruppe FSC® N001967

Printed in Italy
ISBN 978-3-7913-7567-0
www.prestel.com